Author:
Fiona Macdonald studied history at
Cambridge University and at the University of
East Anglia. She has taught in schools, adult
education and universities and is the author of
numerous books for children on historical topics.

Artist:
David Antram was born in Brighton, England,
in 1958. He studied at Eastbourne College of Art
and then worked in advertising for fifteen years
before becoming a full-time artist. He has
illustrated many children's non-fiction books.

Series Creator:
David Salariya was born in Dundee, Scotland.
He has illustrated a wide range of books and has
created and designed many new series for
publishers both in the UK and overseas. In 1989,
he established The Salariya Book Company. He
lives in Brighton with his wife, illustrator Shirley
Willis, and their son Jonathan.

Editor: Karen Barker Smith

Assistant Editor: Michael Ford

Published in Great Britain in 2004 by
Book House, an imprint of
The Salariya Book Company Ltd
25 Marlborough Place, Brighton BN1 1UB

S A L A R I Y A

HB ISBN-13: 978-1-904642-07-7
PB ISBN-13: 978-1-904642-08-4

Please visit the Salariya Book Company at:
www.salariya.com
www.book-house.co.uk

A catalogue record for this book is available
from the British Library.

Printed and bound in China.

Printed on paper from sustainable forests.

Reprinted in MMXIII.

Avoid being a Medieval Knight!

The Danger Zone

Written by
Fiona Macdonald

Illustrated by
David Antram

Created and designed by
David Salariya

BOOK HOUSE

Contents

Introduction

You are a young boy living in England towards the end of the medieval period, around the year AD 1400. Your home is in a huge castle, where your father works. He helps manage its vast estates and spends most of his days shut away in his chamber, poring over old documents or checking accounts. Now that you're eight years old, your father wants you to start learning to be a castle official like him. He thinks you should be pleased at the prospect of such a steady career. But you are horrified – that is not what you want to do!

You have always dreamed of becoming a soldier, like the knight who owns the castle. He is a famous fighting man and is one of the king's trusted champions. You admire the knight's strength, skill and his brave deeds in battle. You envy his riches, his shining armour and his wonderful warhorse. He is your hero and you want to follow his example. But how much do you really know about his life? Are you sure you want to be a medieval knight?

Glamourous Knights

To be a Knight:

KNIGHTS are meant to follow rules of good behaviour, called 'chivalry'. They must promise to be:

Gentle

Brave

Before you decide on your future career, check out what you know about knights. They are elite warriors who fight on horseback. They help lead the armies of kings or noble lords. Some are brave and generous, others are cowardly, or cruel. To show respect for their high rank, knights are always called 'Sir'. There have been knights for hundreds of years. They first became important around AD 800.

Generous

Merciful

Pious

Oh, isn't he handsome!

Hands off – he's mine!

...and also courteous, gallant, obedient, patient and persevering!

At that time, kings and lords recruited expert warriors to help them conquer new lands. They called such men 'knights'. But now, in the 15th century, these knights are sometimes replaced by professional soldiers, called 'mercenaries', who will fight for anyone who will pay them.

Handy hint

If you'd prefer a quiet life, you can pay the king a tax called 'scutage' (shield money) to avoid becoming a knight.

Do you have a rich, noble family?

Not everyone can become a knight. You normally need the right family background – it helps if your father and grandfather were knights before you. But men from ordinary families can also be made knights as a reward for bravery in battle. Women cannot become knights, though they often help defend castles from attackers or accompany armies as cooks and nurses. Most knights' families own large estates, given to them long ago by the kings or lords they promised to fight for. In return for this land, knights have many duties, in peacetime as well as in war.

National duties

FIGHTING. You'll have to fight in the king's army and lead your own troop of soldiers in war.

FRIENDSHIP. You'll have to be a good companion to the king and share in all his leisure pursuits.

COUNSELLING. You'll have to offer the king wise advice – even if he doesn't like what you have to say.

Handy hint

Your family will choose a wife to help and support you – whether you like her or not!

Local duties

FARMING. You'll have to manage your family's lands and give orders to the peasants working there.

FINANCE. You'll have to collect royal taxes. That will make you very unpopular with everyone!

LEGAL GUARDIAN. You'll have to protect the local peasants at times of conflict as well as settling quarrels between them.

Time to start training

Are you ready to leave your home and family? It takes many years' training to become a knight and most boys start at the age of eight. Your parents will send you to another castle, belonging to a well-respected knight. He'll teach you many new skills, but he almost certainly won't understand how homesick you'll feel. You'll meet several other boys at his castle, all hoping to be knights, like you. The youngest will work as pages (household servants) and grooms (stableboys). The oldest will serve as squires (personal assistants), taking important messages, carrying weapons, leading horses and helping knights to get ready for battle.

Learning to be a Knight

WAITING AT TABLES and serving food will teach you good manners and neat, nimble habits.

BUILD UP YOUR MUSCLES. Training with heavy wooden swords will make you strong enough to fight with real weapons.

LEARNING TO HUNT with hawks will teach you to observe your surroundings and be a good lookout.

HORSE SENSE. Feeding and grooming large warhorses will teach you how to handle them when it's time to ride off to battle.

C'mon lad. If you want to be a knight you have to leave home.

TARGET PRACTICE.
Riding at a quintain (a target fixed to a swivelling pole with a weight at the other end) will teach you how to fight with a lance (below).

Handy hint

Watch out for bullies! You'll find several bigger boys training at the same castle as you.

Quintain

Lance

Ooof!

11

Loyalty to your lord

Knights are meant to be loyal. They swear oaths (solemn promises) to be faithful to the king and to their lord. The first and most important of these oaths takes place when a squire has completed his training and is ready to become a knight. This usually happens about the age of 21. The evening before the ceremony, he has a bath and puts on clean clothes. Then he goes to the castle chapel and spends the night in prayer. The next morning, he kneels before the king – or his lord – and promises to serve him loyally. The king then dubs (taps) him on the shoulder, saying "Arise, Sir knight."

Arise, Sir Knight.

THE RIGHT ROBES? The king or your lord will give you a uniform, called 'livery', made to his own design. Your squire will help you dress (left).

PICTURE PUZZLE. You will have to learn how to read heraldic designs (right). Each noble family has its own coat of arms, which they'll expect you to recognise.

Be careful if you're chosen to carry a banner into battle. It will make you an easy target for the enemy.

WIN YOUR SPURS! As a new knight, you'll have to prove your courage and skills on the battlefield. Medieval people call this 'winning your spurs'.

Spurs

Only knights fight on horseback and need to wear spurs.

DON'T CHOOSE A LOSER! You'll meet many rival lords (left). Only one can bring you success. Those lords on the wrong 'side' – and the knights serving them – might end up losing their lives!

WANT TO BE PAID TO FIGHT? Then join a band of mercenary soldiers (right). They'll fight for anyone who gives them money.

Life in a castle

Castle conditions

Living in a castle is not always easy, pleasant or comfortable. How could you cope with:

You have spent all your life in other knights' castles. Do you really want one as your own home? Castles are very expensive to build, or dangerously hard work if you want to capture someone else's! Once you have a castle, you must keep it well-repaired and pay for soldiers to guard it night and day. Inside, castles are becoming more cosy than they have been for centuries. You'll find private rooms for you and your family, with fireplaces in most rooms and tapestries hanging on the walls. Most castles are still cold and draughty in winter and horribly smelly in the summer – especially when sewage from the garderobes (lavatories) leaks into the castle moat!

freezing-cold battlements;

rowdy soldiers in their quarters;

a flaming-hot kitchen;

a rising drawbridge;

a noisy, fiery forge;

a fast-falling portcullis;

and a dismal dungeon?

Get Kitted out

 ompared with ordinary foot soldiers, knights are very fortunate. They have armour to protect them in battle. In the past, this was made of chain mail but it is now usually made of 'plates' – shaped pieces of metal, carefully joined together. This new armour looks very impressive, but it is also extremely expensive. As a new knight, you'll probably have to make do with hand-me-downs from your family.

DRESSED TO KILL. You will need help from a squire to put on your armour, but it only takes about 15 minutes. Be careful to fasten all the separate pieces properly, otherwise the result could be disastrous! First of all, put on a padded tunic which includes chain mail sections (1). Attach a chain mail kilt (2). Put on the plate armour, carefully fastening all the straps (3). Finally, add your helmet and gauntlets (4).

Visor to cover face

Breastplate

Chain mail kilt

Gauntlets (gloves)

Greaves (shin guards)

Alternatively, you could buy second-hand armour, or loot some from a dead knight during battle! Whether it's old or new, all armour clanks, creaks and chafes. It's hot and heavy to wear and can slow you down, trip you up, or get in the way of your weapons. Remember – even the best armour is not guaranteed to save you. In battle, you'll always have to fight for your life!

Handy hint

Don't be old-fashioned! Remember, styles of armour change over the years.

Rivet

Metal ring

MAKING A CHAIN MAIL tunic is extremely time-consuming (above). Thousands of separate rings have to be shaped from metal wire, linked with their neighbours, then held in place by rivets. More modern plate armour is a little quicker to create.

17

Armed and dangerous

In battle, you will rely on your weapons. You should own five or six different kinds: a mace, a long sword, a short sword, a battle-axe, a lance and maybe a dagger. All are sharp, awkward and heavy – just one sword will weigh over a kilo – and you must be able to handle them well, without injuring yourself. You will have to decide which weapons to use for defending yourself and which for attacking your enemies. Whichever you choose, act quickly, or an enemy soldier will kill you while you're still making up your mind! The latest lethal weapon is a war hammer, designed to kill knights wearing plate armour by dealing them deadly blows. However, you have to be brave enough to get close to your enemy to hit him!

MACES, or clubs, have heavy metal heads on stout wooden and metal poles.

LONG SWORDS have sharp, double-edged blades and large handles for a good grip. Use them to slash at enemy foot soldiers.

SHORT SWORDS have small blades, with sharp tips. Use them to stab enemy knights through chinks in their armour.

BATTLE-AXES have wedge-shaped blades and short wooden handles. Use them for slicing through foot soldiers' long pikes and leather garments.

Phew – that was close!

Coping on Crusade

Since 1096, European soldiers, known as 'Crusaders', have been fighting in the Holy Land – the area around the city of Jerusalem. Crusaders hope to win this land from the Muslims who have ruled it since AD 637. More recently, there have been Crusades in north-east Europe to force pagan peoples living there into becoming Christians. Most Crusaders do not return from the Holy Land but die, either on the journey or from sickness, or are killed by Muslim soldiers. These troops fight in a way that you've never seen before, shooting at the marching Crusading armies with bows and arrows before galloping away!

A dangerous journey...

EXPECT TO FEEL SICK as you sail to the Holy Land, especially if this is your first long journey by sea.

TRY NOT TO WORRY about being shipwrecked. Only a few of the Crusaders' ships sink on each voyage!

DON'T GET STUCK in a snowdrift as you cross the mountains. Dig yourself out quickly, or you'll die of cold!

Handy hint

The Holy Land is hot! Copy Muslim soldiers and wear a loose surcoat over your armour. It will help you keep cool!

to a dangerous place

KEEP FLEAS OUT of your tent in the Holy Land. They carry the germs that cause plague, which can kill you!

STAY AWAY FROM SNAKES! Most are not deadly poisonous, but their bites can be very painful.

DON'T RUN OUT OF WATER in the desert. Always carry plenty with you, or you'll die of thirst!

Surviving a siege

Sieges are sometimes the only way to capture castles or walled cities. You need patience – and huge war machines – to carry out a successful siege. You must organise your army to surround the enemy city or castle and give them orders to stop anyone from entering or leaving. Then you have to wait, until the supplies of food and water run out inside and the inhabitants either starve or surrender. If you are particularly cunning or cruel you might torture enemy captives outside the walls, to warn defenders what will happen if they don't give in.

Germ warfare

SPREAD SICKNESS by polluting enemy water supplies with the rotting corpses of dead animals. Germ-laden dead bodies can also be hurled over enemy walls.

CLEVER 'CAT' (moveable shed). This shelters sappers – soldiers digging tunnels under enemy walls to make them crumble and collapse.

TREBUCHET.
When one end is pulled down, the other shoots up and flings rocks high over enemy defences.

Keep up the bombardment men! Their defences won't hold for much longer.

BRUTAL BATTERING RAM. Made of a huge tree trunk and tipped with iron, a battering ram is strong enough to smash holes in gates and crack stonework.

BIG BELFRY – that's what the soldiers call this tall siege tower. From the top, they can shoot arrows at defenders on the battlements.

MURDEROUS MANGONEL. This huge catapult can hurl huge lumps of rock through the air. Its power comes from ropes twisted tightly, then released.

23

Bravery in battle

Look out for:

GUNNERS, who try to kill you with shot (stone or metal balls); longbowmen, who try to kill you with sharp, feathered arrows; and crossbowmen, who try to kill you with metal bolts.

Gun (used from c. 1400)

Longbow

Crossbow

n battle, you'll face many different types of fighters, as well as other knights. Most enemy troops ranged against you will be foot soldiers. They make up the majority of most medieval armies and are recruited from rough, tough peasants. Many such soldiers are angry at being ordered away from their fields by their king or lord.

They want to win battles quickly and then go home, which can make them vicious enemies! Compared with knights, most foot soldiers are only part-time fighters, but this does not make them any less dangerous. They are armed with various types of deadly weapons, including pikes, pitchforks and wooden clubs. Their bows shoot bolts and arrows that fall like 'killer rain' on the enemy, including you!

Handy hint

Bind up wounds with egg-soaked bandages and stop bleeding by cauterising wounds with a red-hot iron.

Don't fall off your horse!

A knight's most important possessions are his warhorses. Fierce stallions, called 'destriers' and 'coursers', are specially bred for battle. Warhorses must be extremely strong, to carry knights plus their weapons and armour. By nature they are aggressive and they are also trained to bite and kick. A good warhorse is very expensive and you'll need at least two! Knights also need pack-horses to carry baggage and riding horses for squires and grooms.

IN BATTLE, you line up alongside other knights, holding your lance 'couched' (braced) against your side. When you dig your spurs into his side, your horse will charge towards the enemy!

Beware!

STAY AWAY FROM STAKES! Half buried, pointing upwards, these sharp wooden poles kill many horses and riders.

CHAAARGE!

Caltrops

BEWARE OF BOGS! Don't let damp, soggy ground trap you and your horse and sink your chance of victory.

PREPARE FOR PITS! Your enemies will dig pits, then cover them with leaves or grass ready for you to fall into.

BE CAREFUL OF CALTROPS! These iron spikes, scattered on the ground, cruelly dig into horses' hooves.

Handy hint

A high-backed saddle and long stirrups will help you stay on your horse.

Aaargh!

27

So many ways to die...

rom the start of your training as a knight, your life will be at risk. It's hard to know for sure, but most fighting men die before they are 50 years old. All knights hope to be remembered after they die. Many pay artists to create lifelike portraits of them, to be displayed in the church where they will be buried. They pay priests to say prayers and give money to charity so that poor people will remember them gratefully. If you plan on becoming a knight, do as others do and order your tomb straight away!

Try not to...

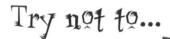

DIE IN BATTLE, in pain and surrounded by the enemy.

DIE FROM INFECTED WOUNDS, a miserable, lingering death.

DIE FROM DYSENTERY, an awful sickness.

DIE IN PRISON, locked in chains, then abandoned.

and try to...

DIE FROM HEATSTROKE, half cooked inside your armour.

DIE FROM FROSTBITE, shivering and chilled to the bone.

BE SEVERELY INJURED and unable to work for the rest of your life.

DIE PEACEFULLY IN YOUR BED. That is actually how many retired knights end their days!

Glossary

Banner A flag carried by a knight who commanded other knights.

Bolt A short arrow, fired by a crossbow.

Caltrops Sharp metal spikes, scattered in front of horses, to wound them and stop them advancing.

Cauterise To burn body tissue in order to seal it and stop bleeding.

Chivalry Rules of good behaviour that all knights were meant to follow.

Coat of arms Badge worn by a knight, to show he belonged to a noble family.

Courteous Polite and considerate.

Crusades Wars fought between Christians and Muslims for the right to rule the Holy Land.

Dub To tap on the shoulder with a sword. It is part of the ceremony of becoming a knight.

Dysentery An infectious disease that causes terrible sickness and diarrhoea.

Elite Best, or highest-ranking.

Gallant Brave, unselfish and romantic.

Garderobes Lavatories. The word means 'guard clothes' – medieval people believed that the smell from lavatories kept away insects that ate woollen cloth.

Heraldic Belonging to heraldry – the study of coats of arms.

Livery Uniform worn by soldiers fighting in the same knight's army.

Medieval Belonging to the Middle Ages (the years from around AD 1000 to AD 1500).

Mercenary soldiers (or **mercenaries**) Soldiers who fought for anyone who would pay them.

Page A young boy who worked as a servant in a noble family's household.

Persevering Refusing to give in when faced with danger or difficulty.

Pike An axe-shaped metal blade plus a sharp metal spike fitted to the end of a long pole.

Pious Deeply religious and devoted to the Christian Church.

Pitchfork A huge, two-pronged fork on the end of a long pole, usually used as a farming tool.

Plague A deadly disease, also known as the Black Death, caused by bacteria (germs) that were passed from rats to humans by fleabites.

Plate armour Armour made from pieces of metal, carefully shaped and fitted together.

Portcullis Metal gate that dropped down to bar the entrance to a castle.

Quintain Device used for practice fighting. It was made of a swivelling wooden pole with a target at one end and a heavy weight at the other.

Scutage Tax paid by men from rich or noble families who did not want to become knights.

Spurs Sharp spikes, fixed to the heel-pieces of a knight's footwear. They were pressed into a horse's side to make it run more quickly.

Squire A young man who worked as personal assistant to a knight.

Surcoat Long loose robe worn on top of armour. Often decorated with a knight's coat of arms.

Tournaments Mock battles fought by knights for fun and as training for war.

Index